Marriott Edgar

THE LION
and ALBERT

with pictures by
Caroline Holden

METHUEN · LONDON

This edition first published in Great Britain 1978
by Methuen Children's Books Ltd
11 New Fetter Lane, London EC4P 4EE
Reprinted 1982
Text copyright © 1933 Francis, Day & Hunter Ltd
Illustrations copyright © 1978 Caroline Holden
This illustrated edition copyright © 1978 Methuen Children's Books Ltd

Printed in Great Britain by
Blantyre Printing & Binding Ltd
Glasgow and London
ISBN 0 416 58450 0 *(hardback)*
ISBN 0 416 86810 X *(paperback)*

There's a famous seaside place called Blackpool,
　That's noted for fresh air and fun,
And Mr and Mrs Ramsbottom
　Went there with young Albert, their son.

Boys and Gulls

A grand little lad were young Albert,
   All dressed in his best; quite a swell
With a stick with an 'orse's 'ead 'andle,
   The finest that Woolworth's could sell.

They didn't think much to the Ocean:
　The waves, they was fiddlin' and small,
There was no wrecks and nobody drownded,
　Fact nothing to laugh at at all.

So, seeking for further amusement,
 They paid and went into the Zoo,
Where they'd Lions and Tigers and Camels,
 And old ale and sandwiches too.

Some photographs that Albert took!

Albert took this one too

Albert's the one on the left

There were one great big Lion called Wallace;
  His nose was all covered with scars—
He lay in a somnolent posture
  With the side of his face on the bars.

Now Albert had heard about Lions,
   How they was ferocious and wild—
To see Wallace lying so peaceful,
   Well, it didn't seem right to the child.

So straightway the brave little feller,
　　Not showing a morsel of fear,
Took his stick with the 'orse's 'ead 'andle
　　And pushed it in Wallace's ear.

Albert playing with the Lion

You could see that the Lion didn't like it,
  For giving a kind of a roll,
He pulled Albert inside the cage, with 'im,
  And swallowed the little lad 'ole.

The Lion playing with Albert

Then Pa, who had seen the occurrence,
And didn't know what to do next,
Said, "Mother! Yon Lion's ate Albert,"
And Mother said, "Eee, I am vexed!"

Then Mr and Mrs Ramsbottom—
 Quite rightly, when all's said and done—
Complained to the Animal Keeper
 That the Lion had eaten their son.

The keeper was quite nice about it;
He said, "What a nasty mishap.
Are you sure it's *your* boy he's eaten?"
Pa said, "Am I sure? There's his cap!"

Zoo keeper and friends

The manager had to be sent for.
  He came and said, "What's to do?"
Pa said, "Yon Lion's ate Albert,
  And 'im in his Sunday clothes, too."

Then Mother said, "Right's right, young feller;
   I think it's a shame and a sin
For a lion to go and eat Albert,
   And after we've paid to come in."

The manager wanted no trouble,
   He took out his purse right away,
Saying, "How much to settle this matter?"
   And Pa said, "What do you usually pay?"

But Mother had turned a bit awkward
   When she thought where her Albert had gone.
She said, "No! Someone's got to be summonsed,"—
   So that was decided upon.

Outside the police station

Then off they went to the P'lice Station,
  In front of the magistrate chap;
They told 'im what happened to Albert,
  And proved it by showing his cap.

Some pictures at the police station

The lost property room

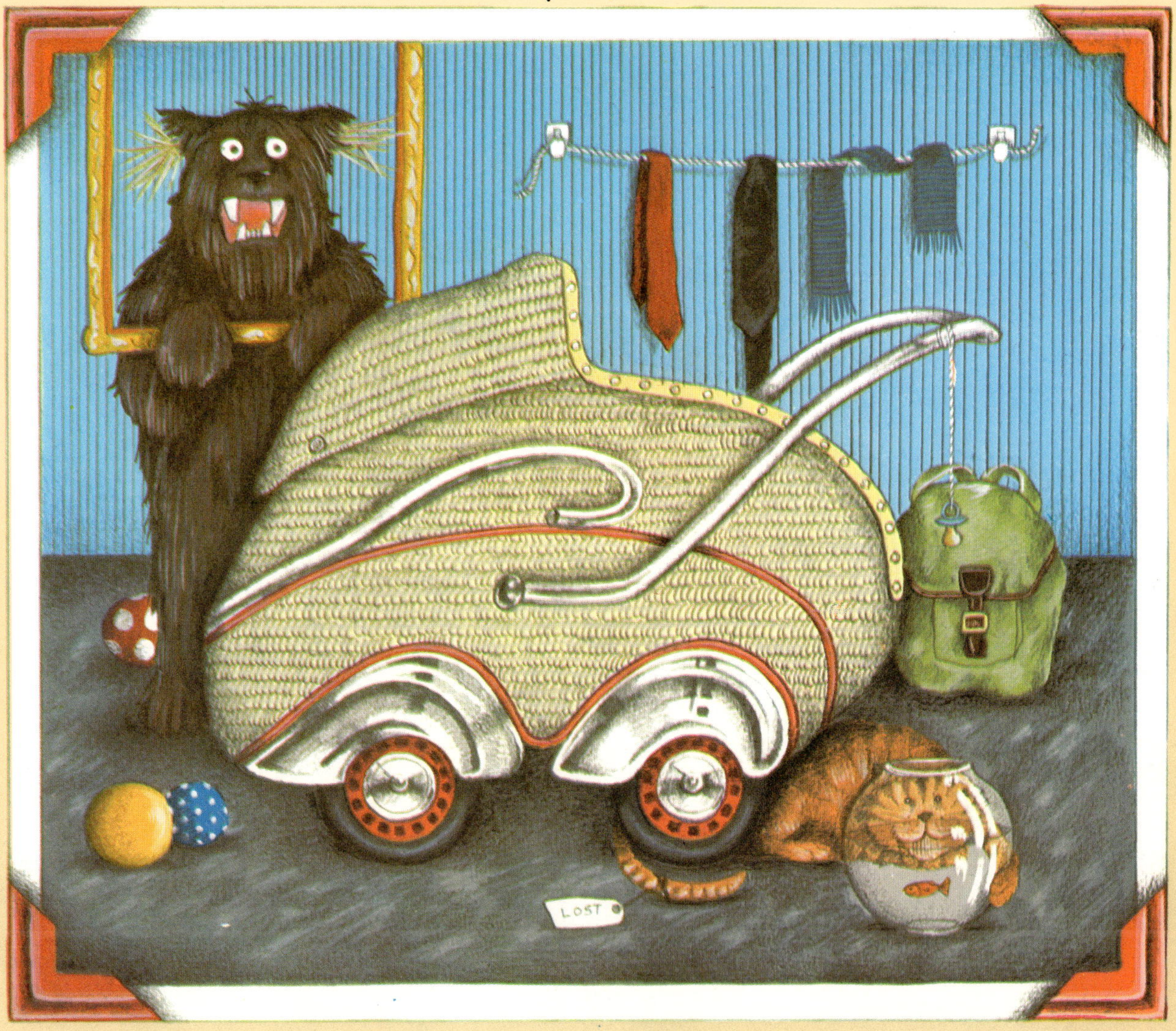
LOST

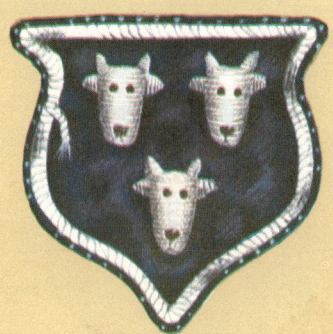

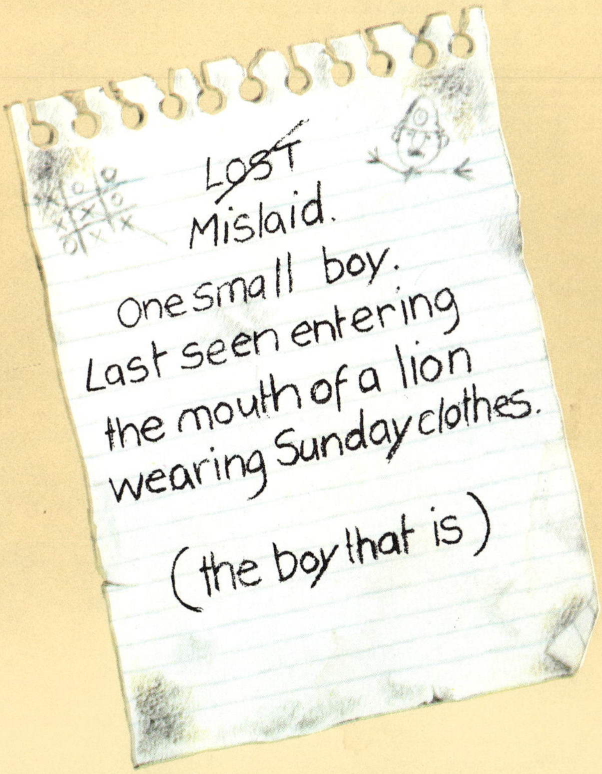
~~LOST~~
Mislaid.
One small boy.
Last seen entering
the mouth of a lion
wearing Sunday clothes.
(the boy that is)

Albert's school badge

The Magistrate gave his opinion
　That no-one was really to blame
And he said that he hoped the Ramsbottoms
　Would have further sons to their name.

At that Mother got proper blazing,
　"And thank you, sir, kindly," said she.
"What, waste all our lives raising children
　To feed ruddy Lions? Not me!"